AF587871

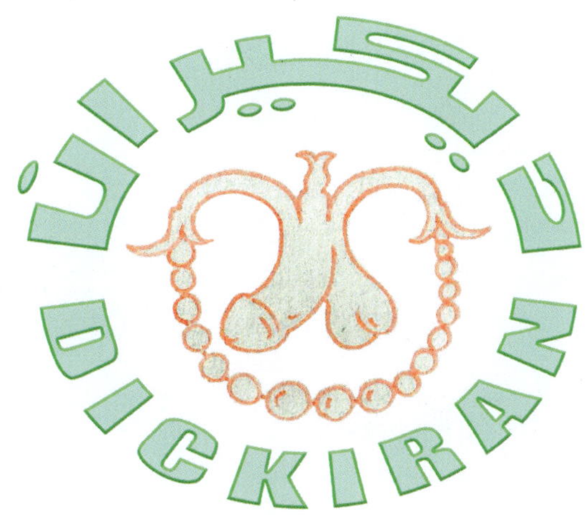
DICKIRAN

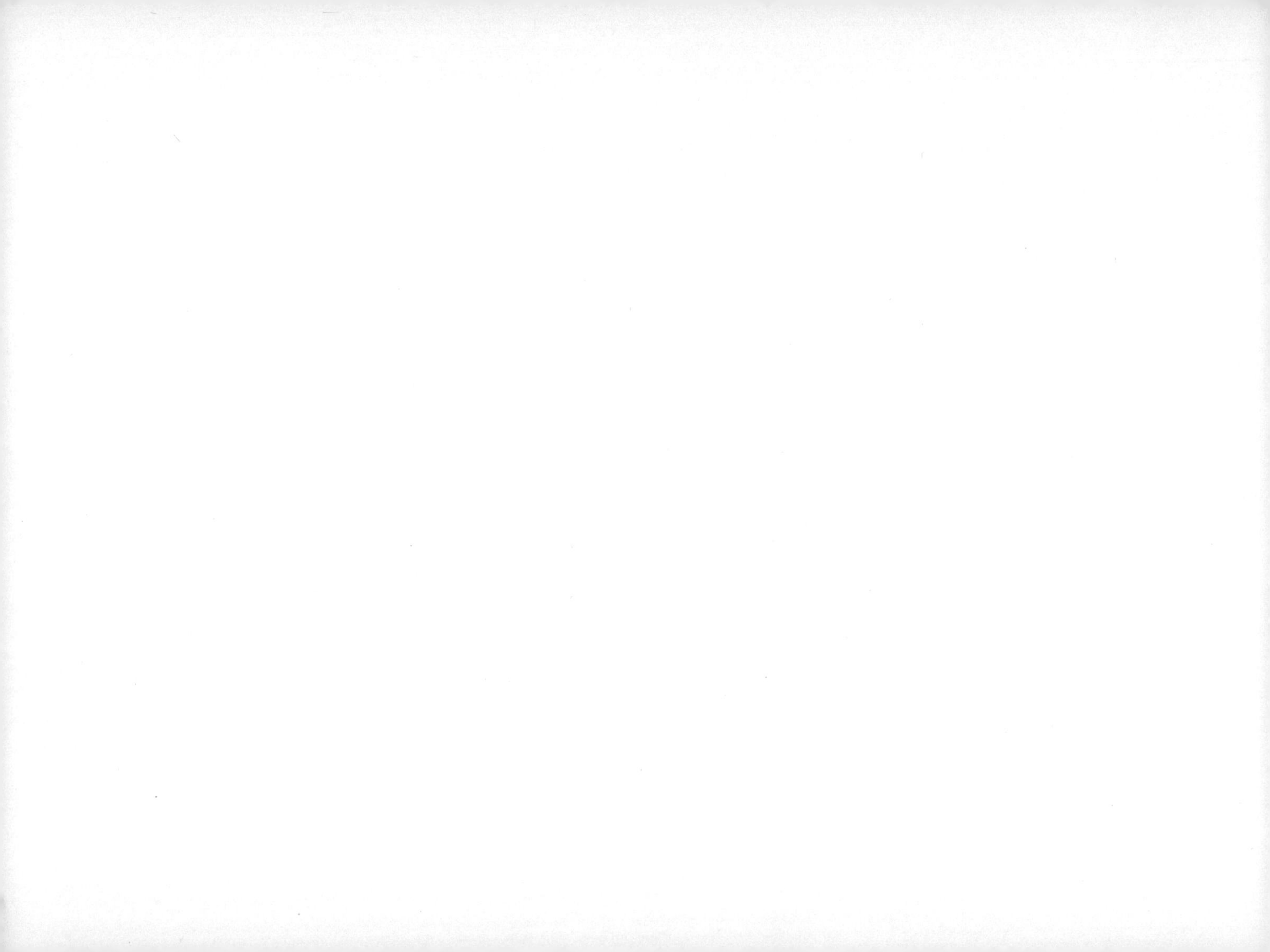

D I C K I R A N

By Baktash

During the pandemic I started surfing websites that I used to visit when I was a teenager. One of them was Looti, an illegal Iranian pornographic forum, with a diverse range of sexual topics including my favorite one "Iranian dicks and balls forum".

I started collecting pictures of Iranian men's dicks, which they were uploading to this forum since 2007. I collected more than 600 dick pics and then started drawing a selection of them on sandwich papers. I drew 13 and then put a pause on the project until summer 2023, when I added 16 more dicks to the collection.

The collection that you'll see in this book includes 29 drawings of these selected dick pictures, divided into two chapters: The pandemic, and Summer 2023. Hope you enjoy!

Baktash

I

The Pandemic

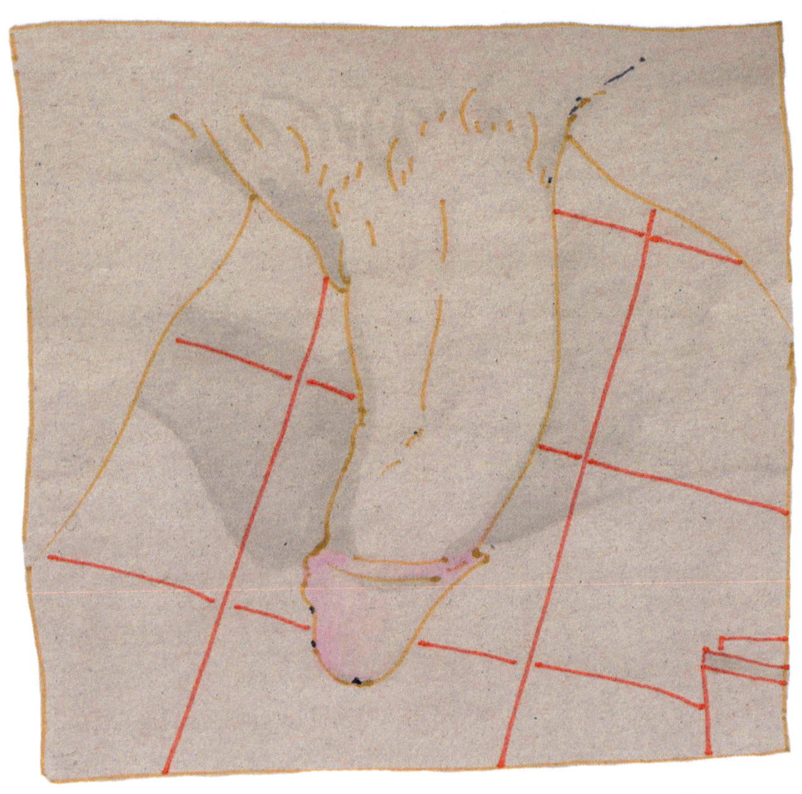

Lunch Time

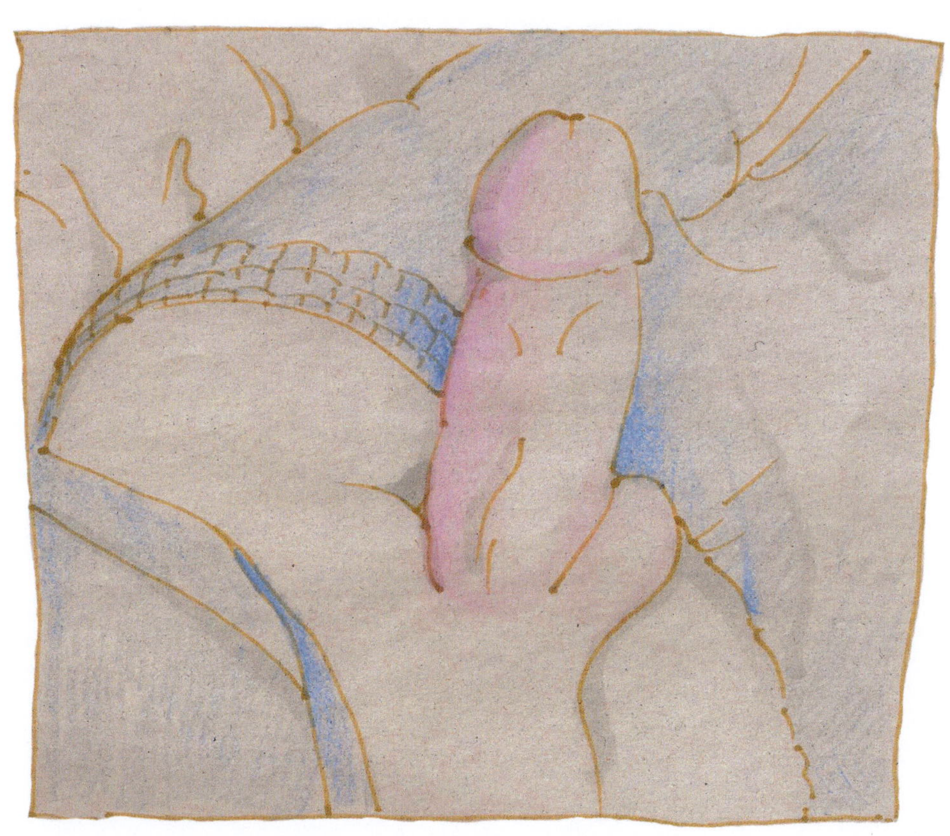

Good Morning

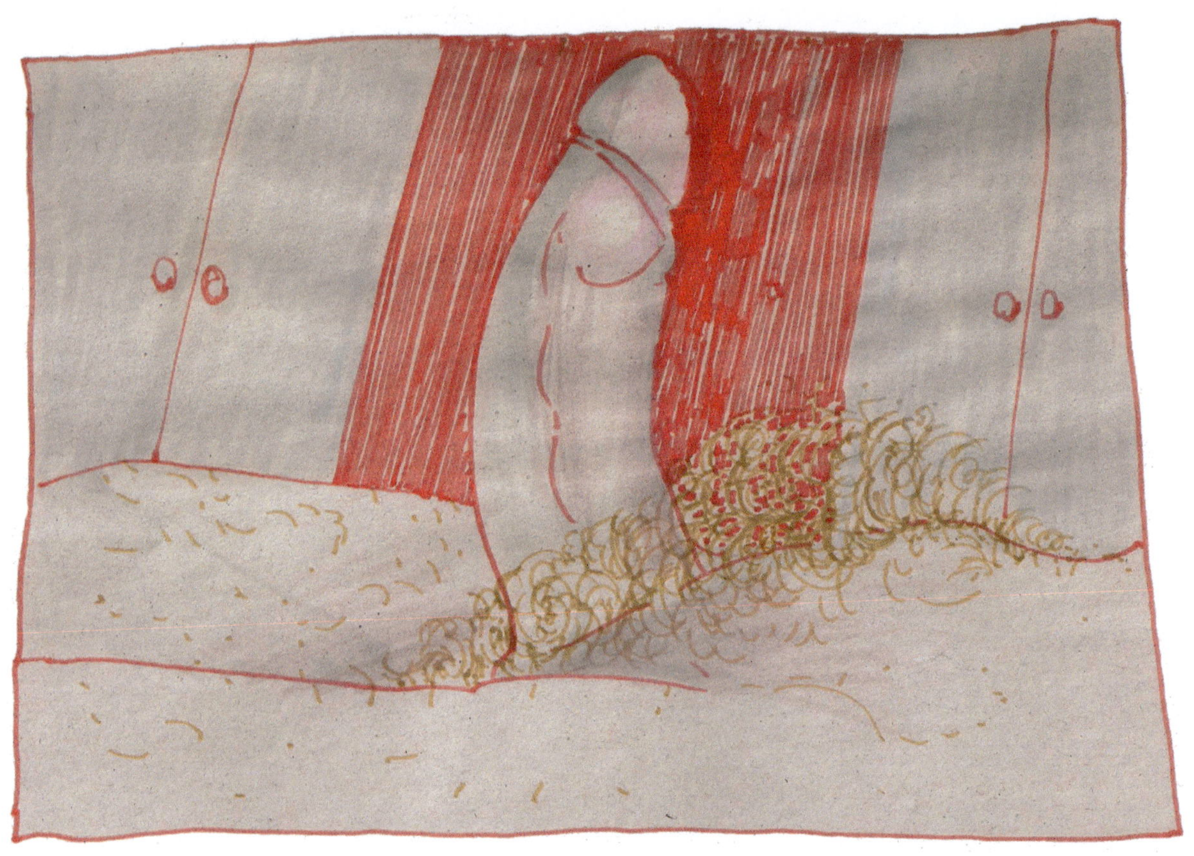

Out of the Closet

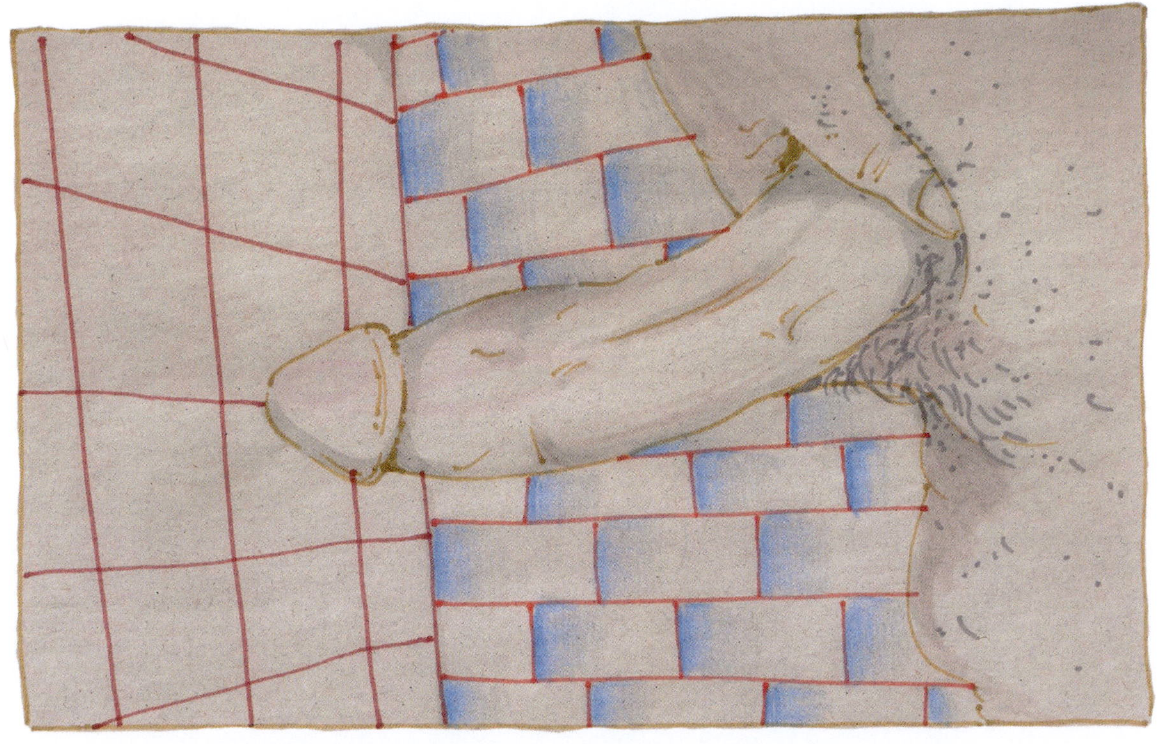

Bath House Memories

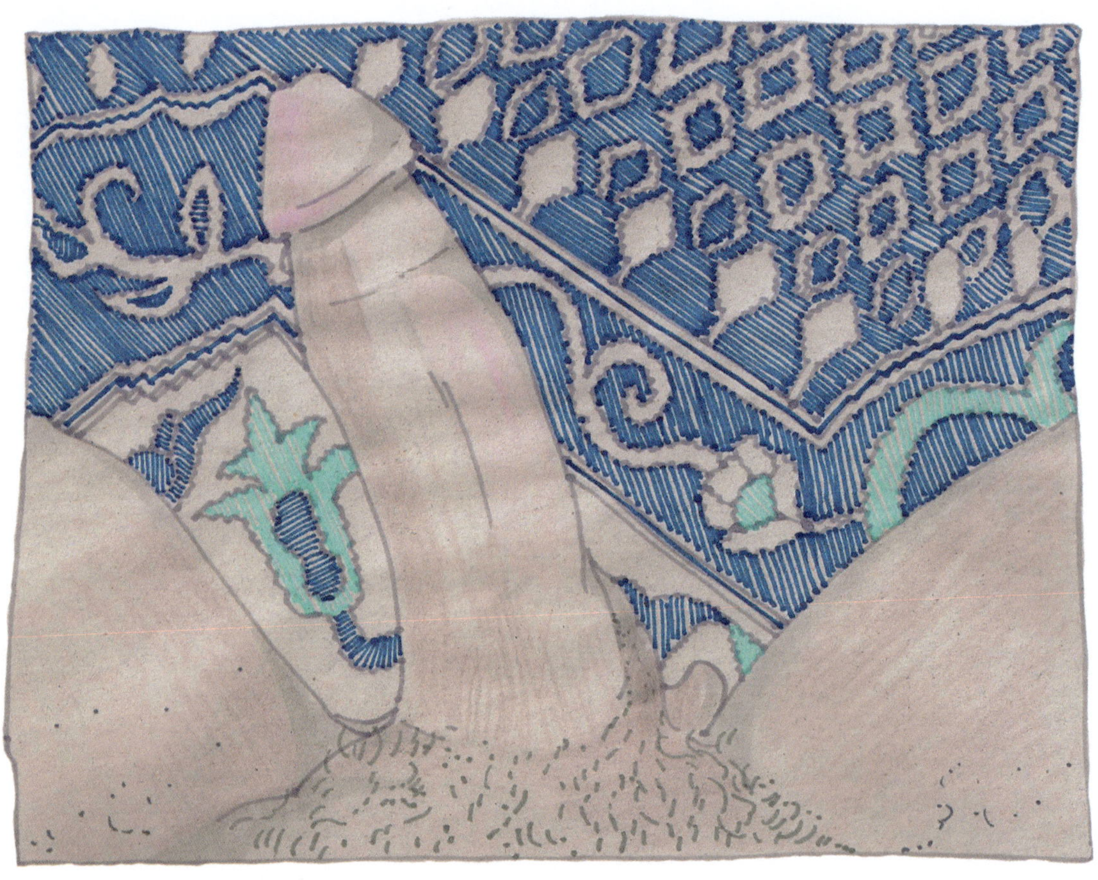

Picnic Behind the Scene

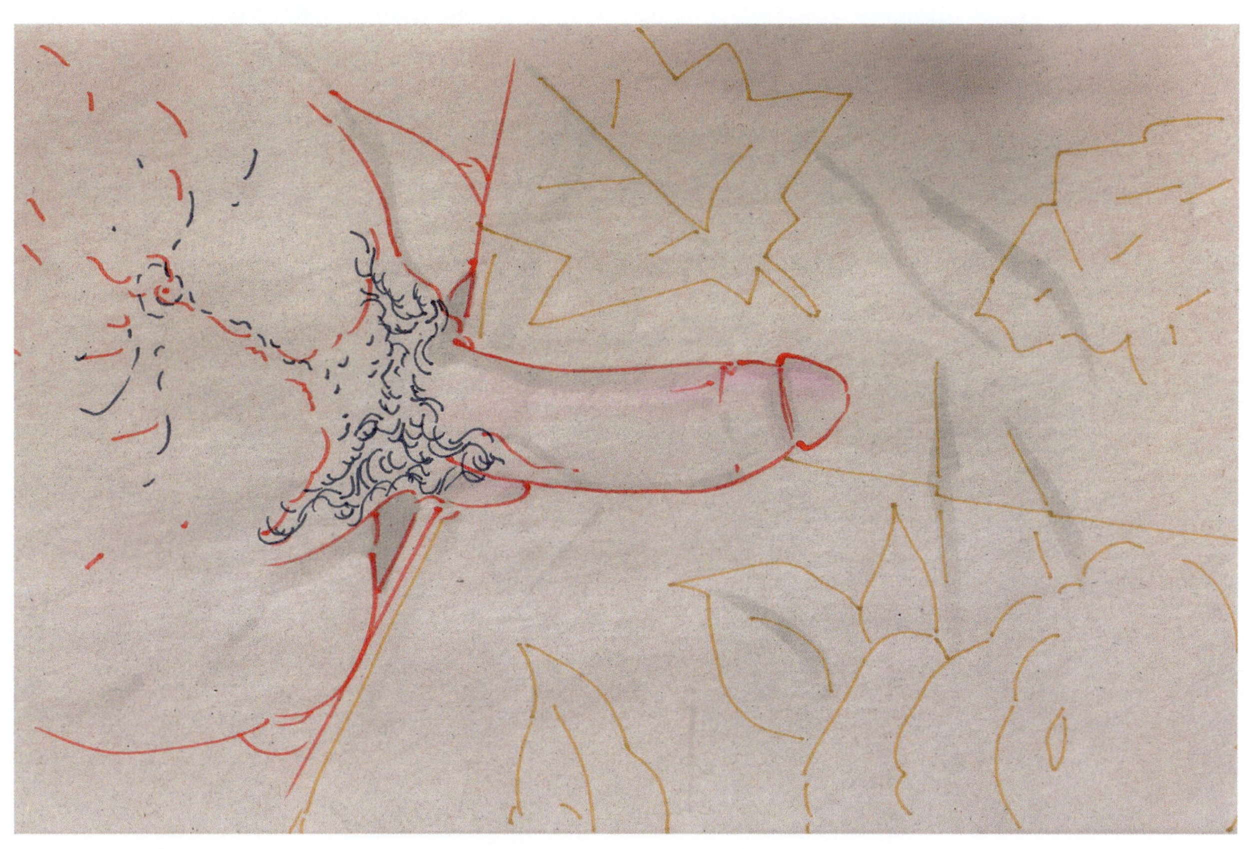

Bedroom POV

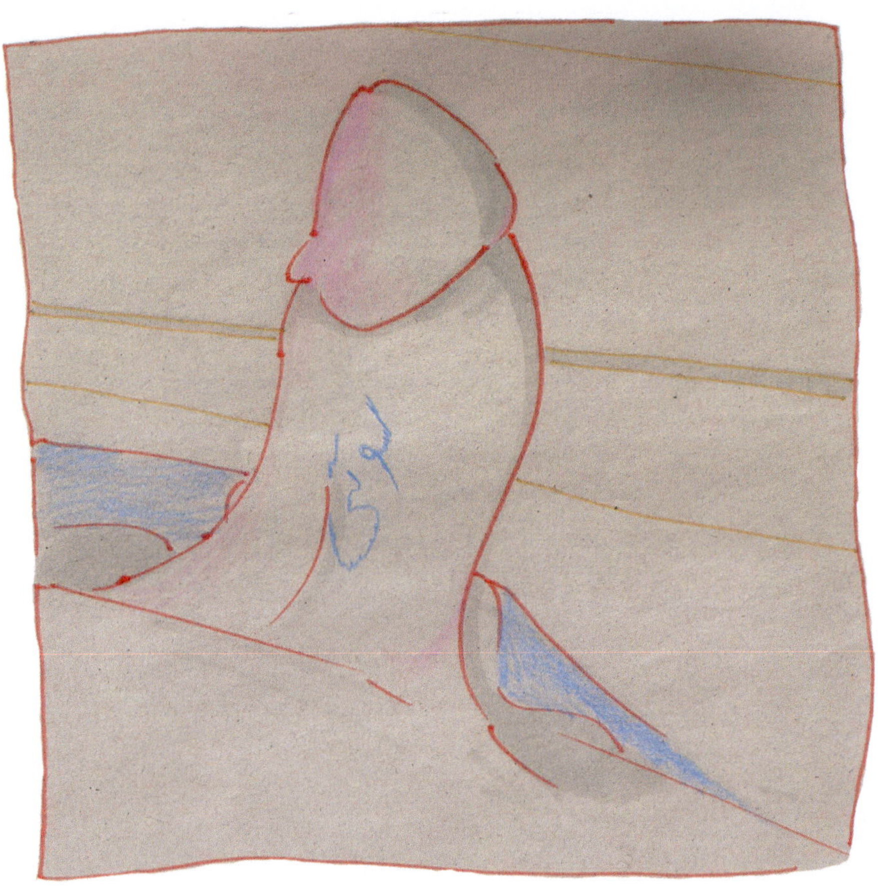

"Looti"

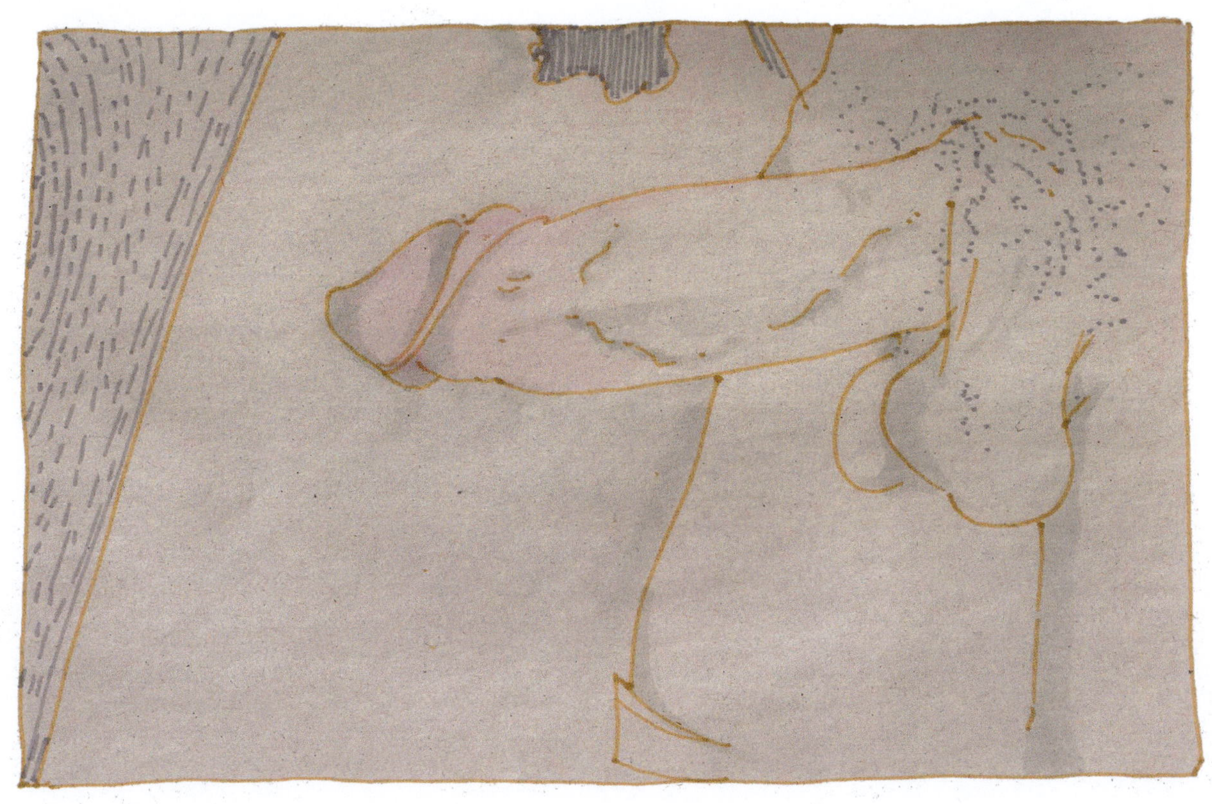

The Sandwich

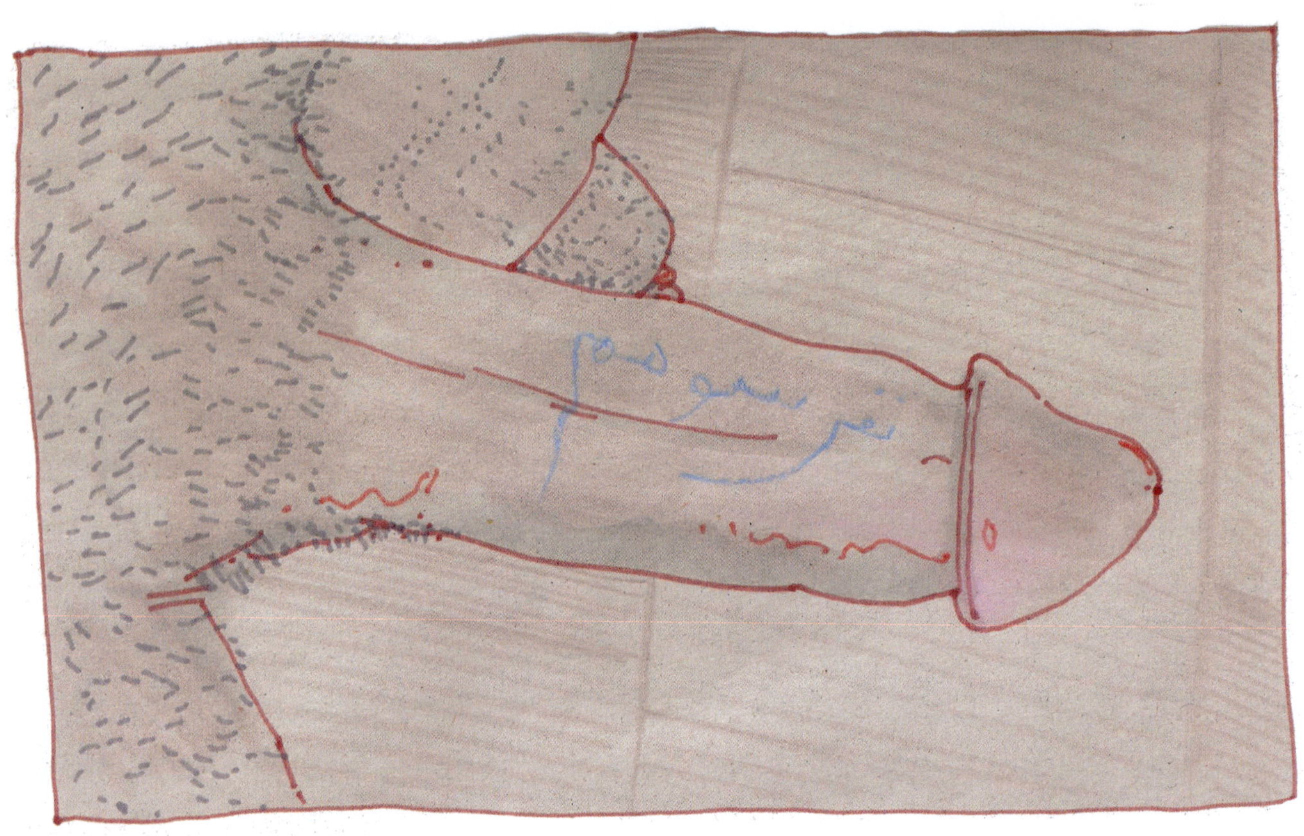

"Third"

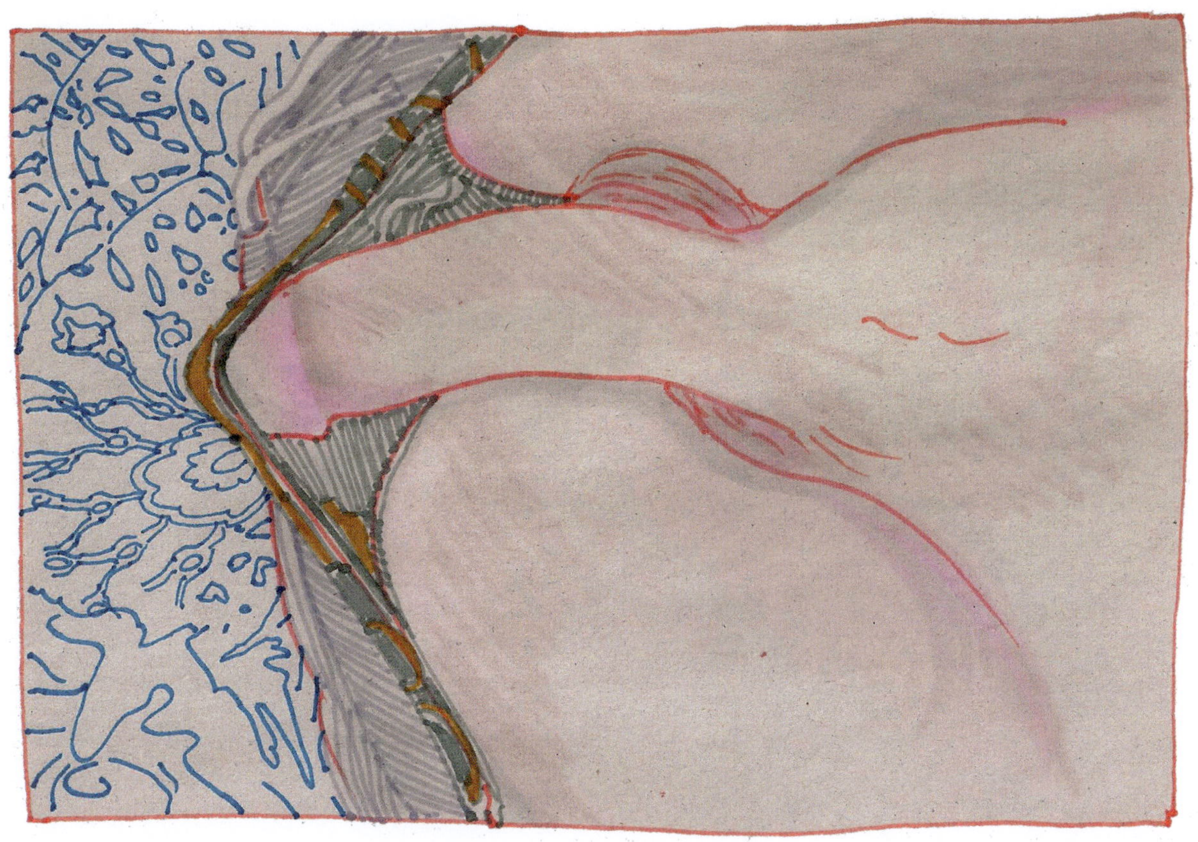

Waking Up

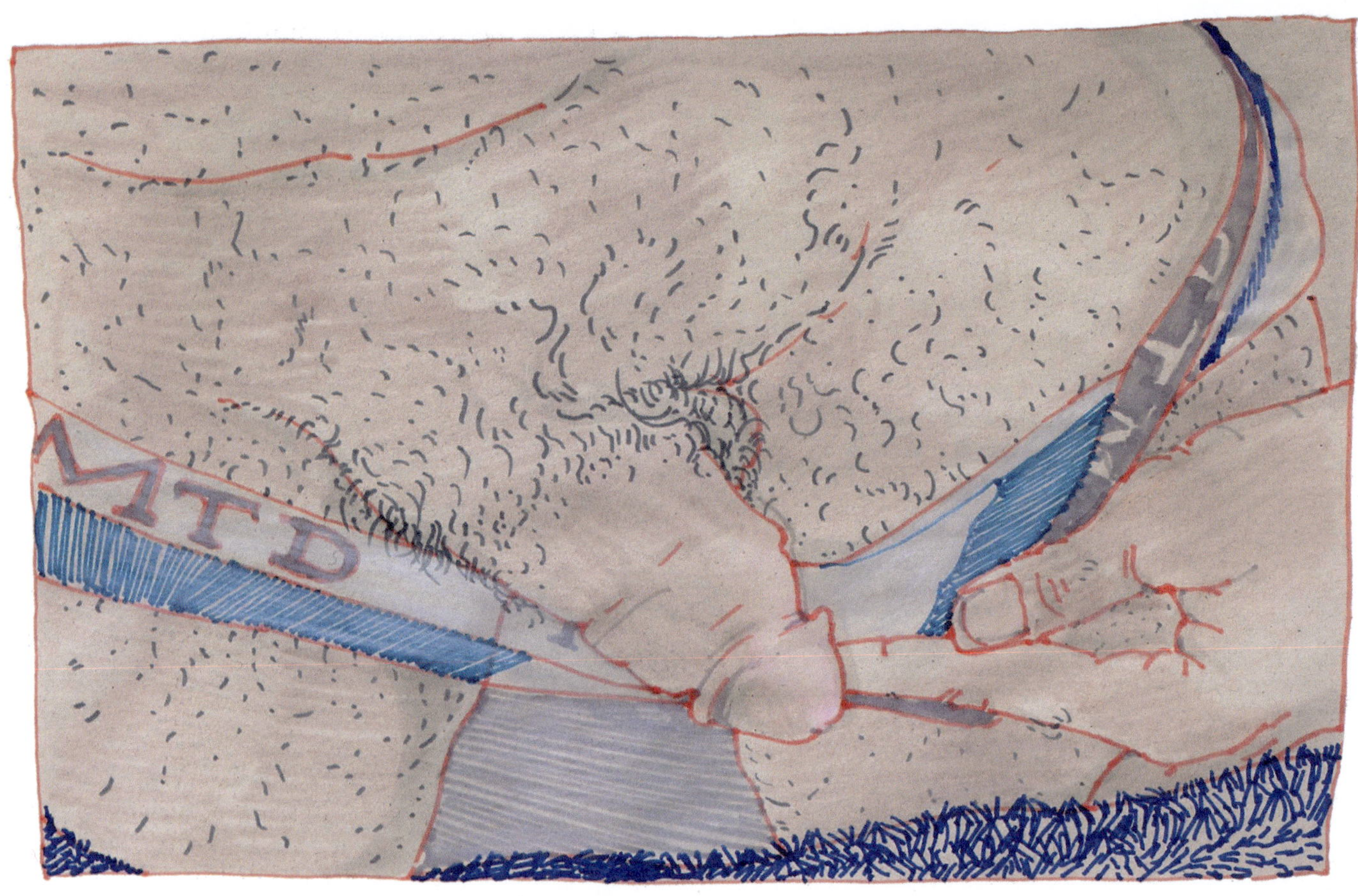

Sleepy Worm

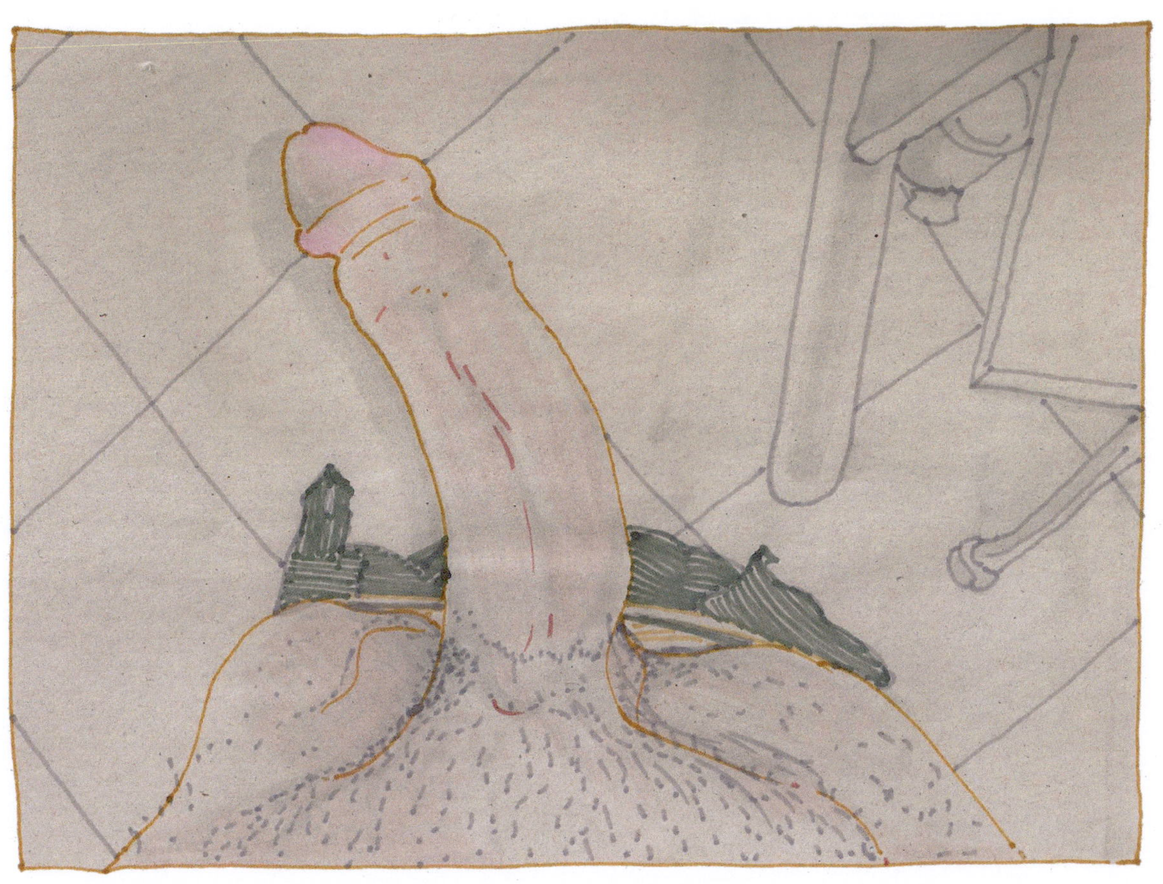

Men at Work

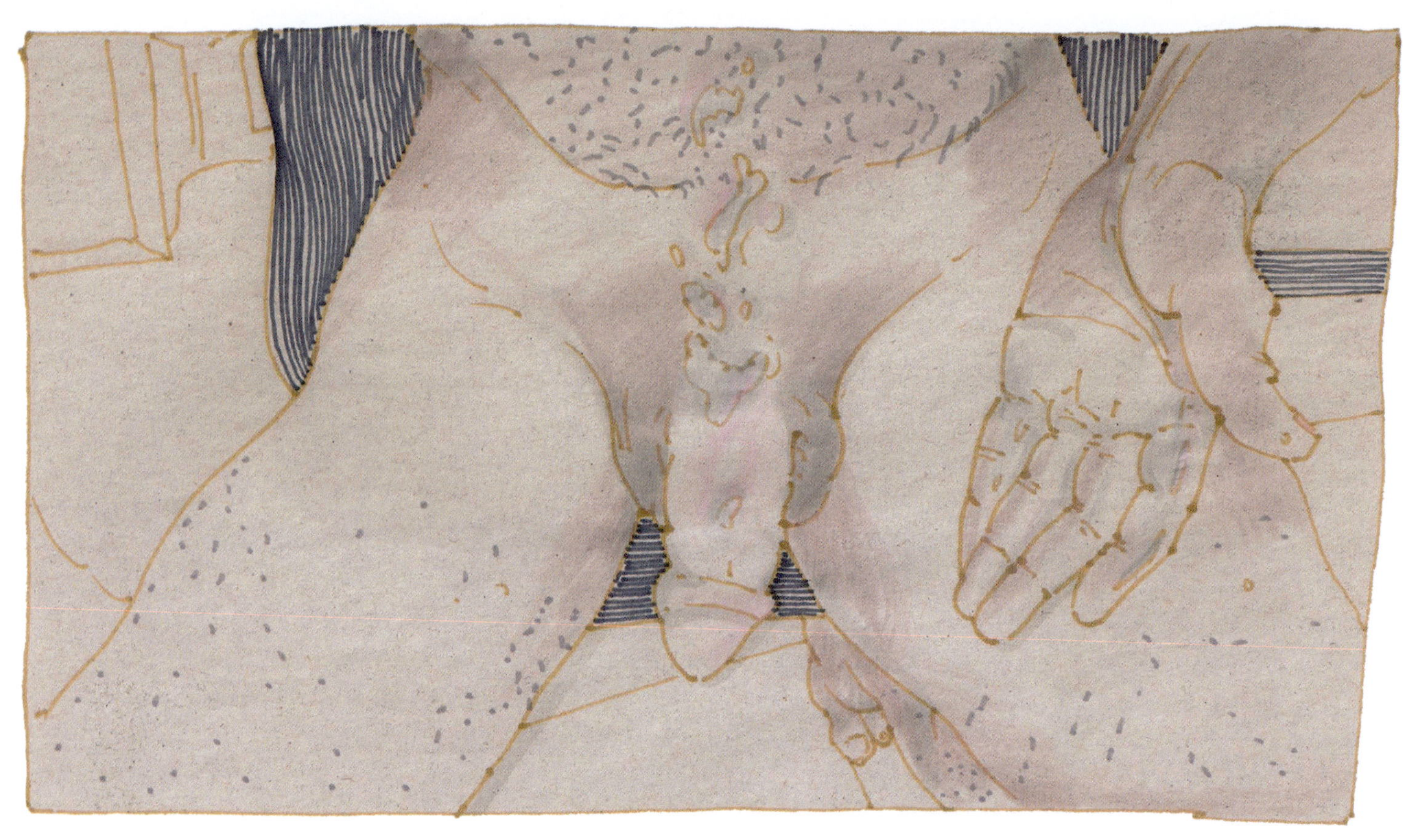

Breakfast

II

Summer 2023

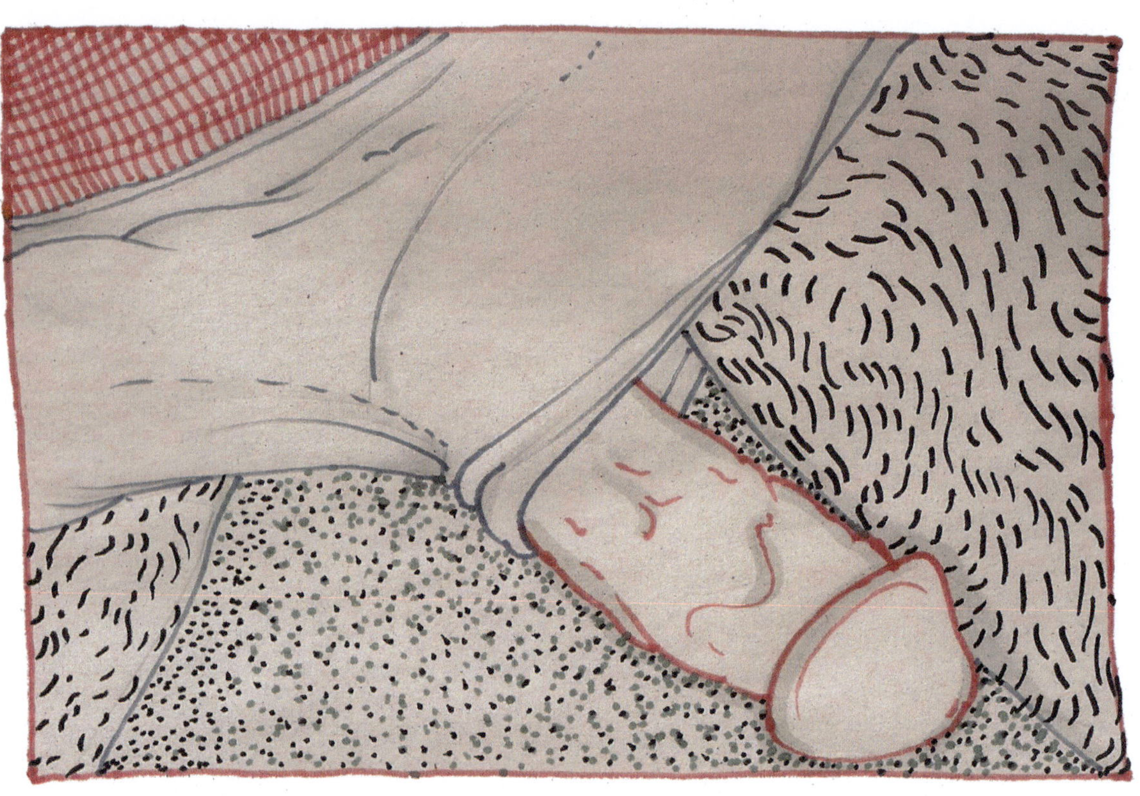

Magic Wand

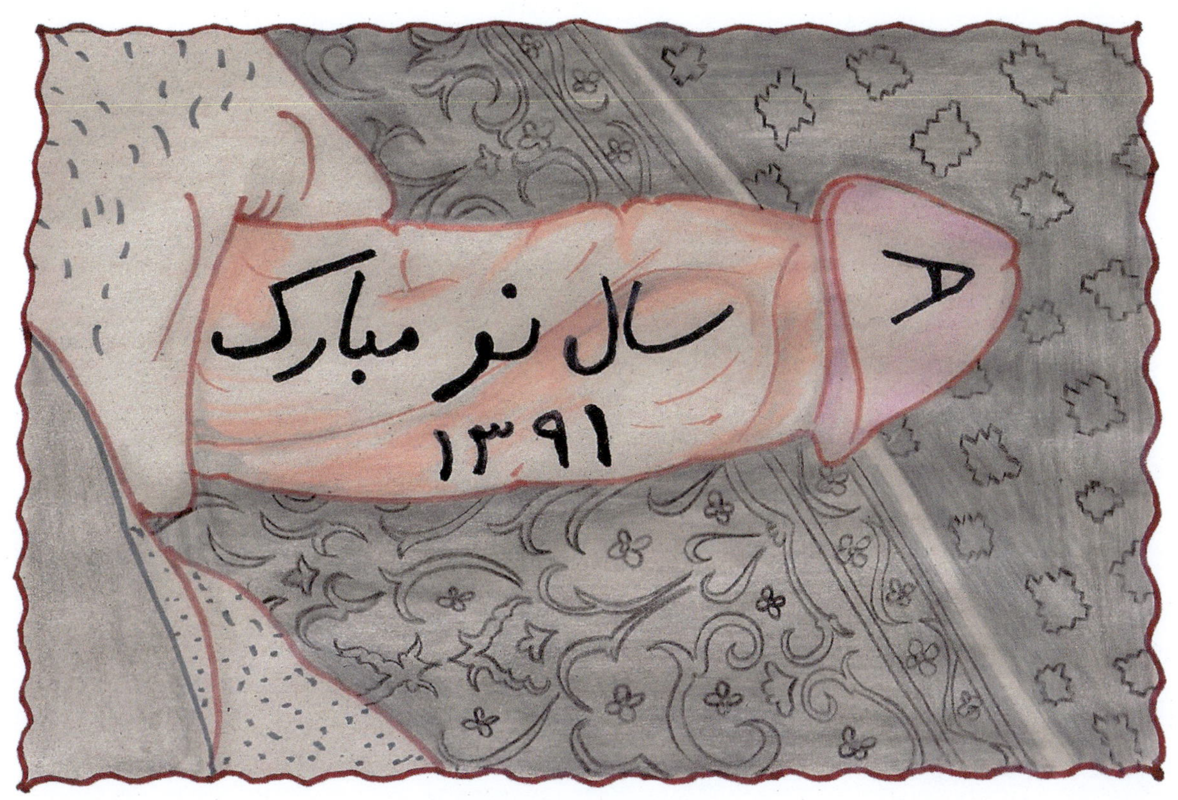

Happy New Year

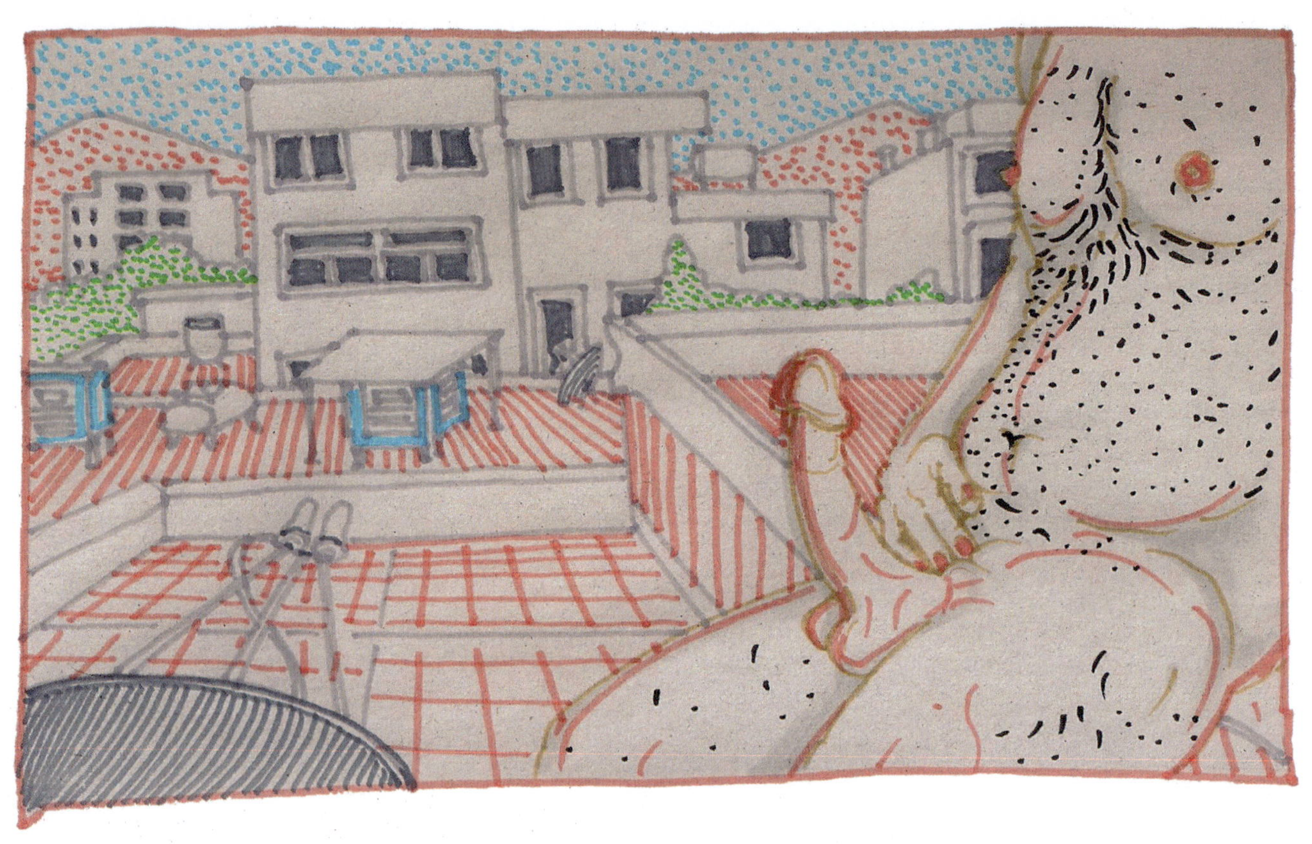

Tehran from the Rooftop

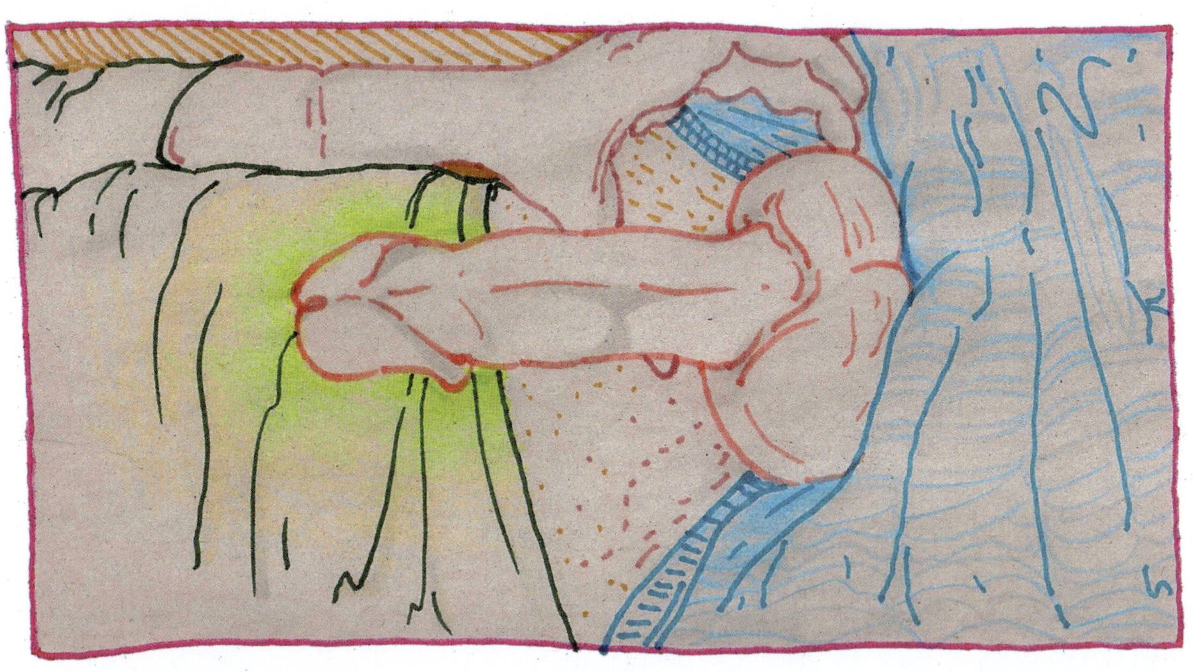

Nap Time POV

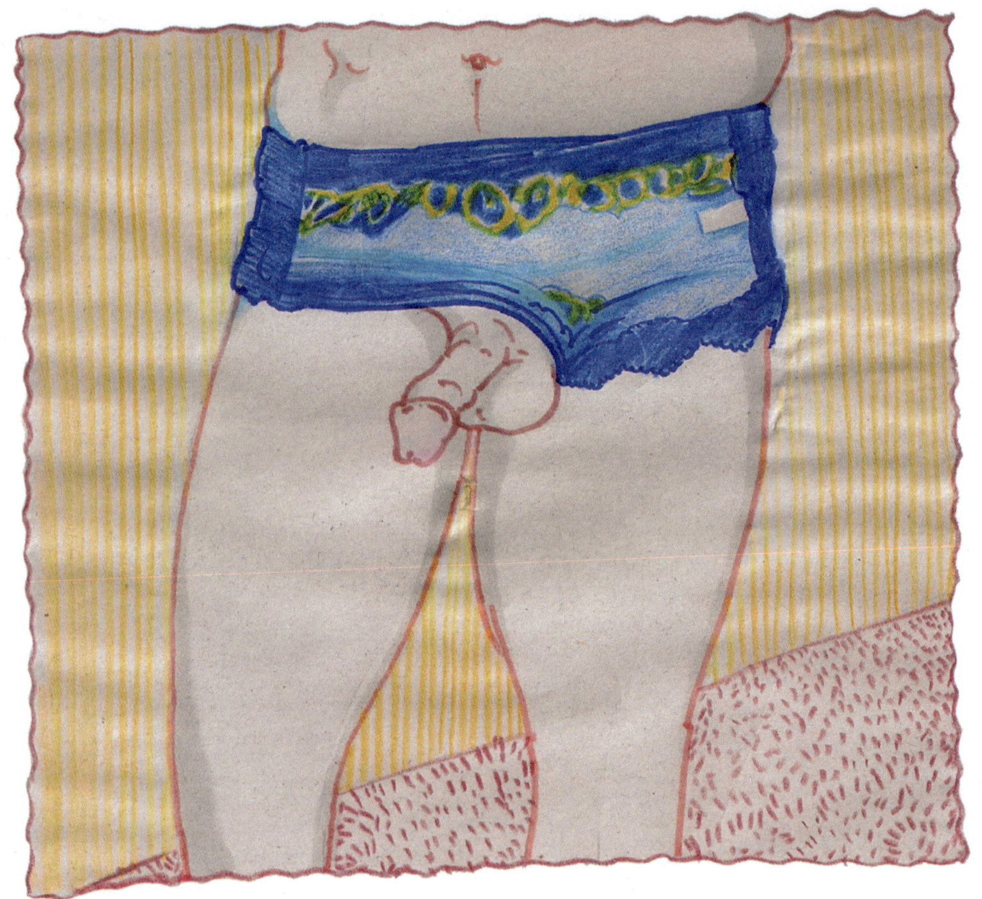

Dancer in the Light

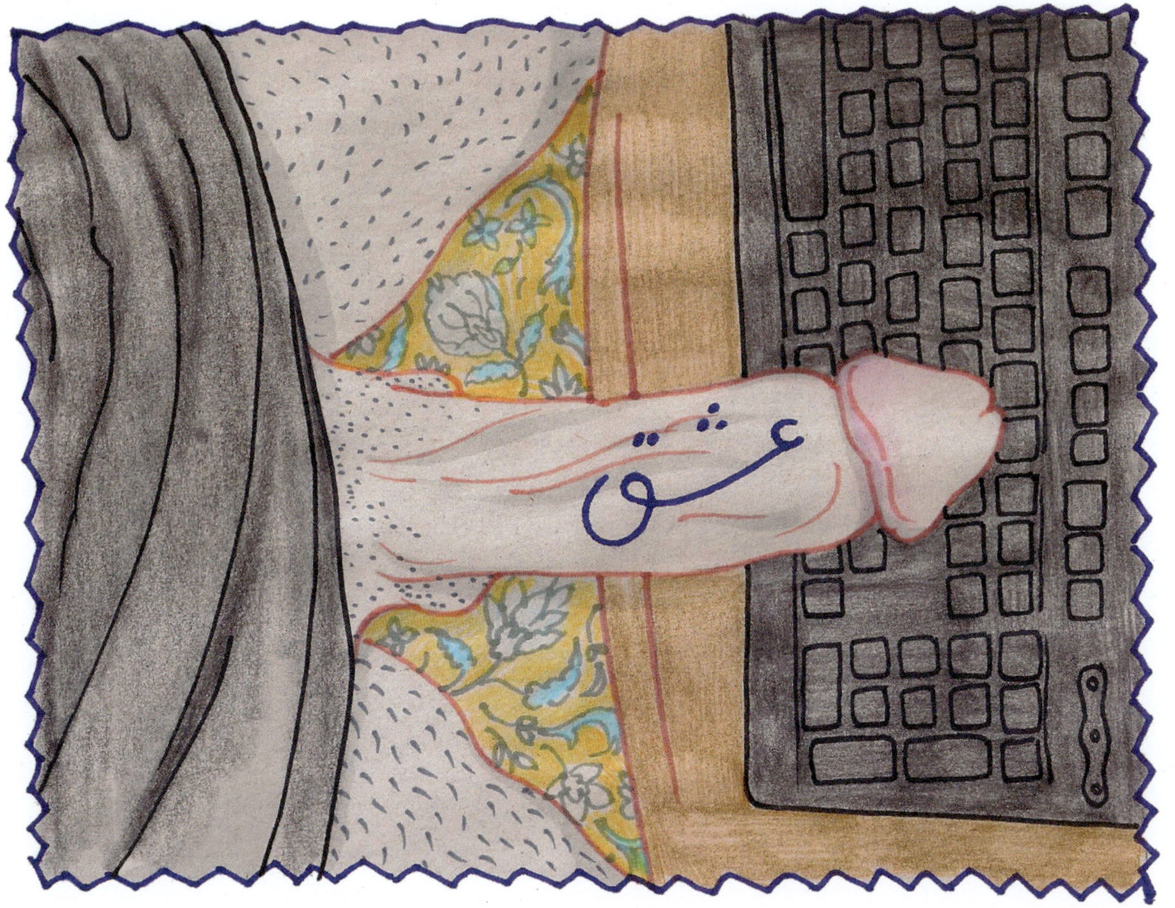

“Love”

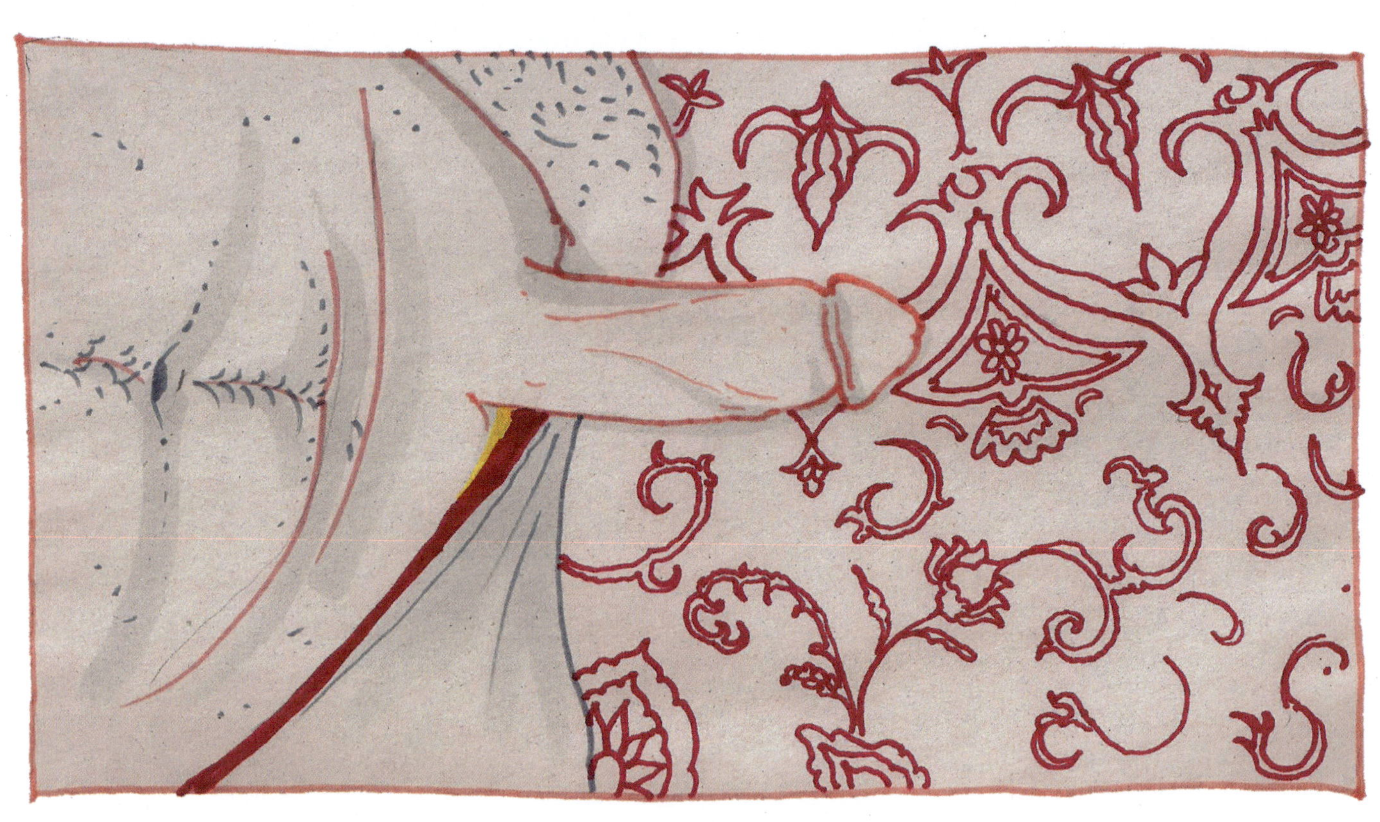

Smells Like a Wild Garden

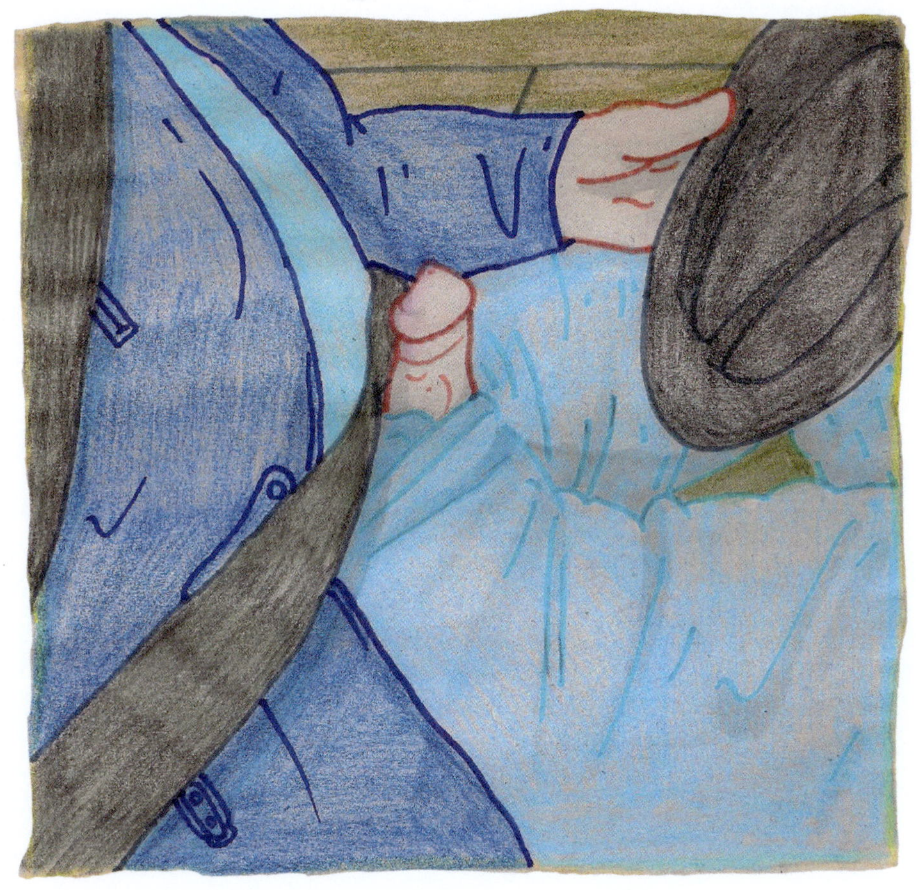

Only Me and My Taxi Driver

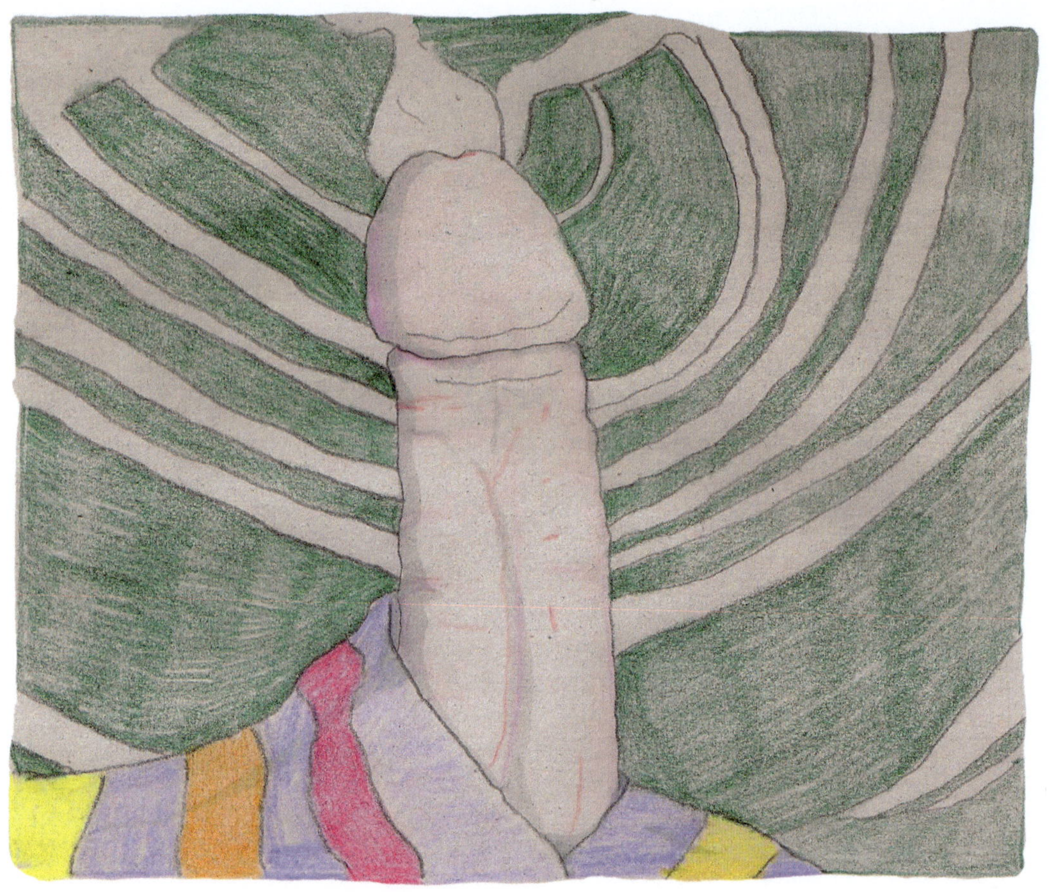

Put Your Shirt On

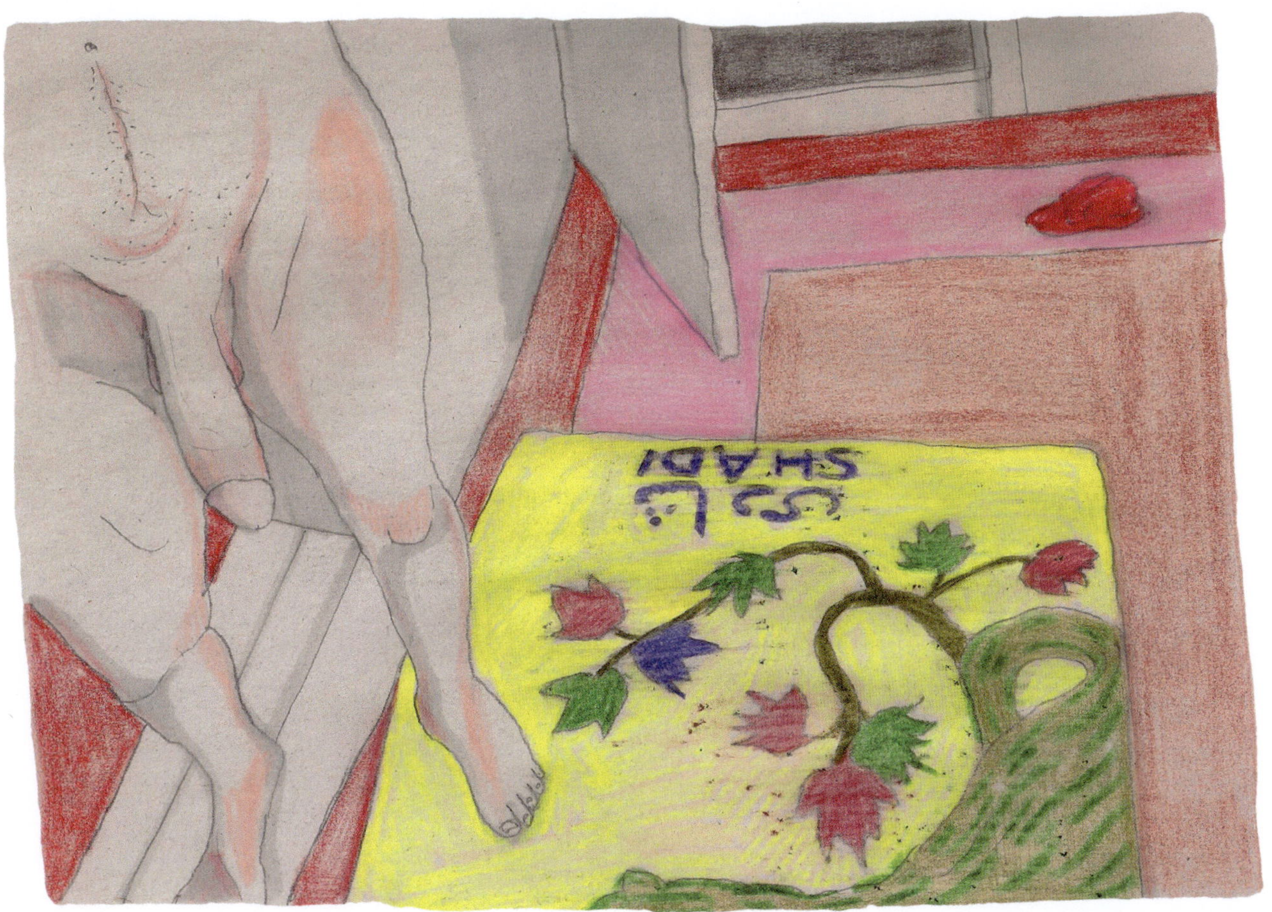

Happiness Blanket

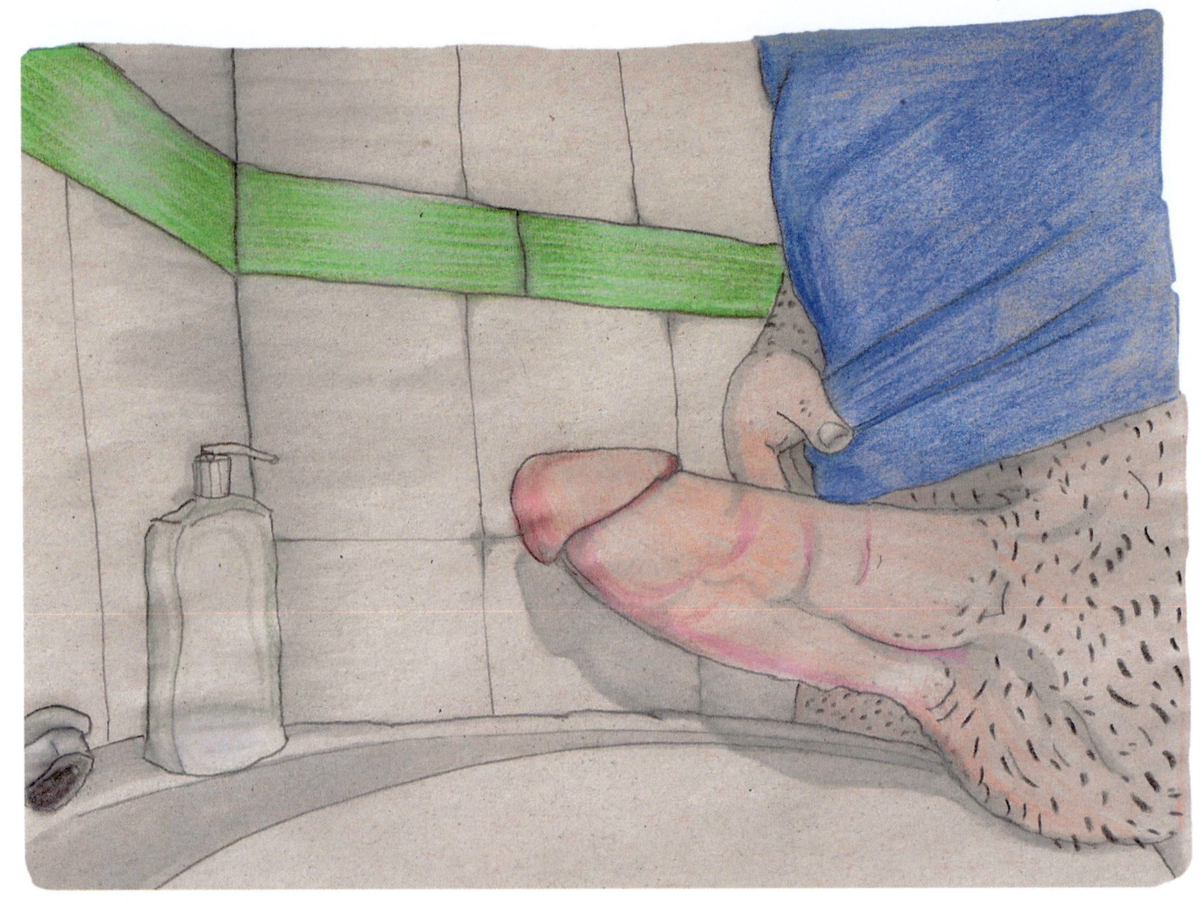

Before Washing Your Face

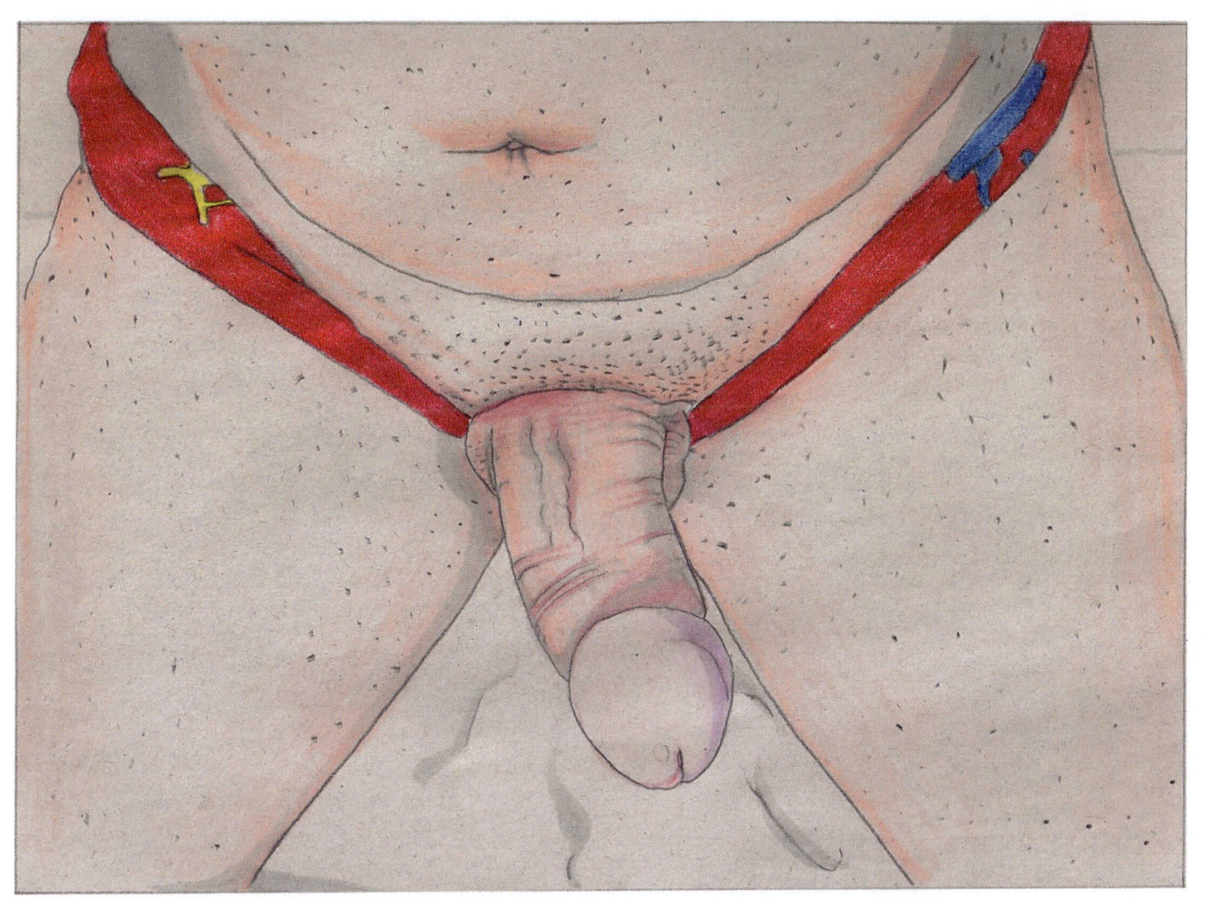

Waiting for a Kiss

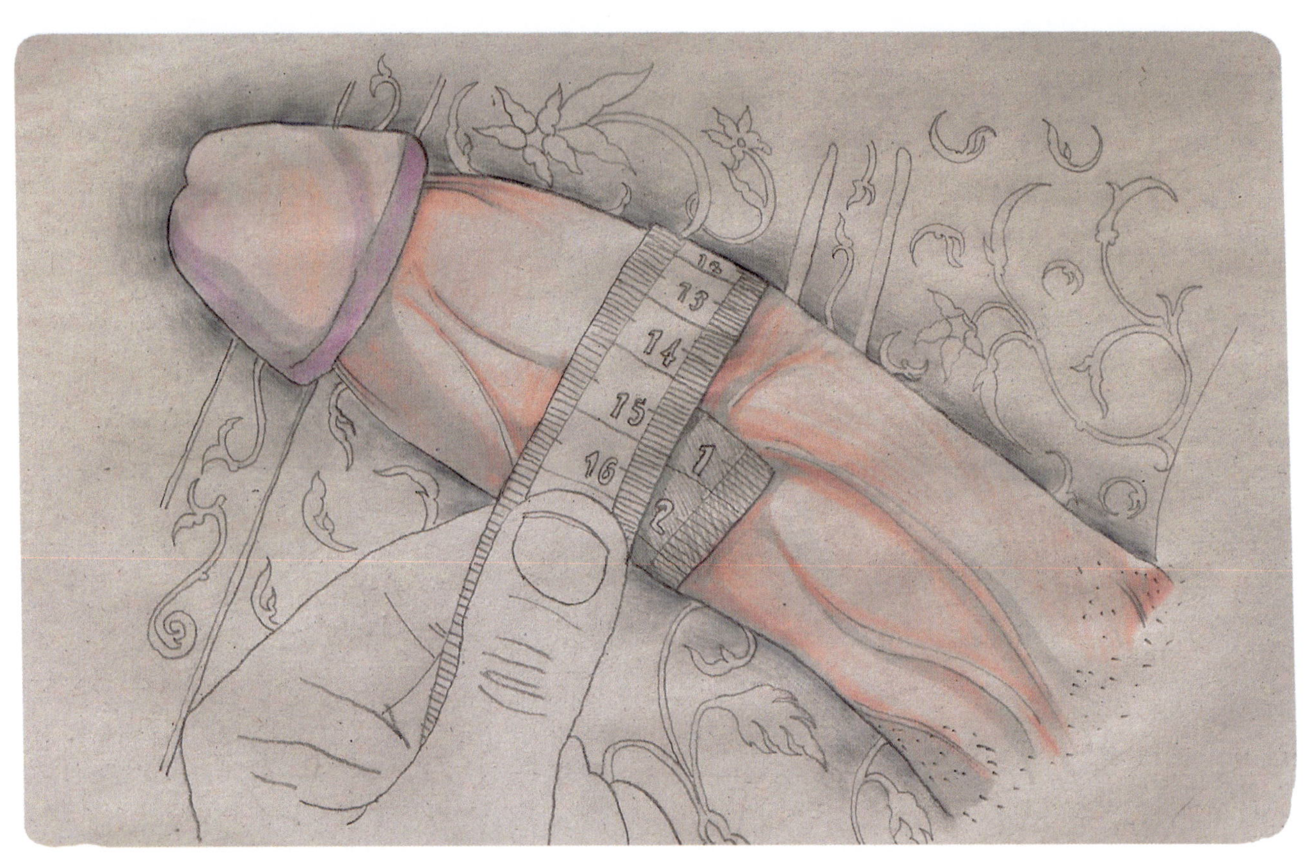

Show Me How Much You Love Me

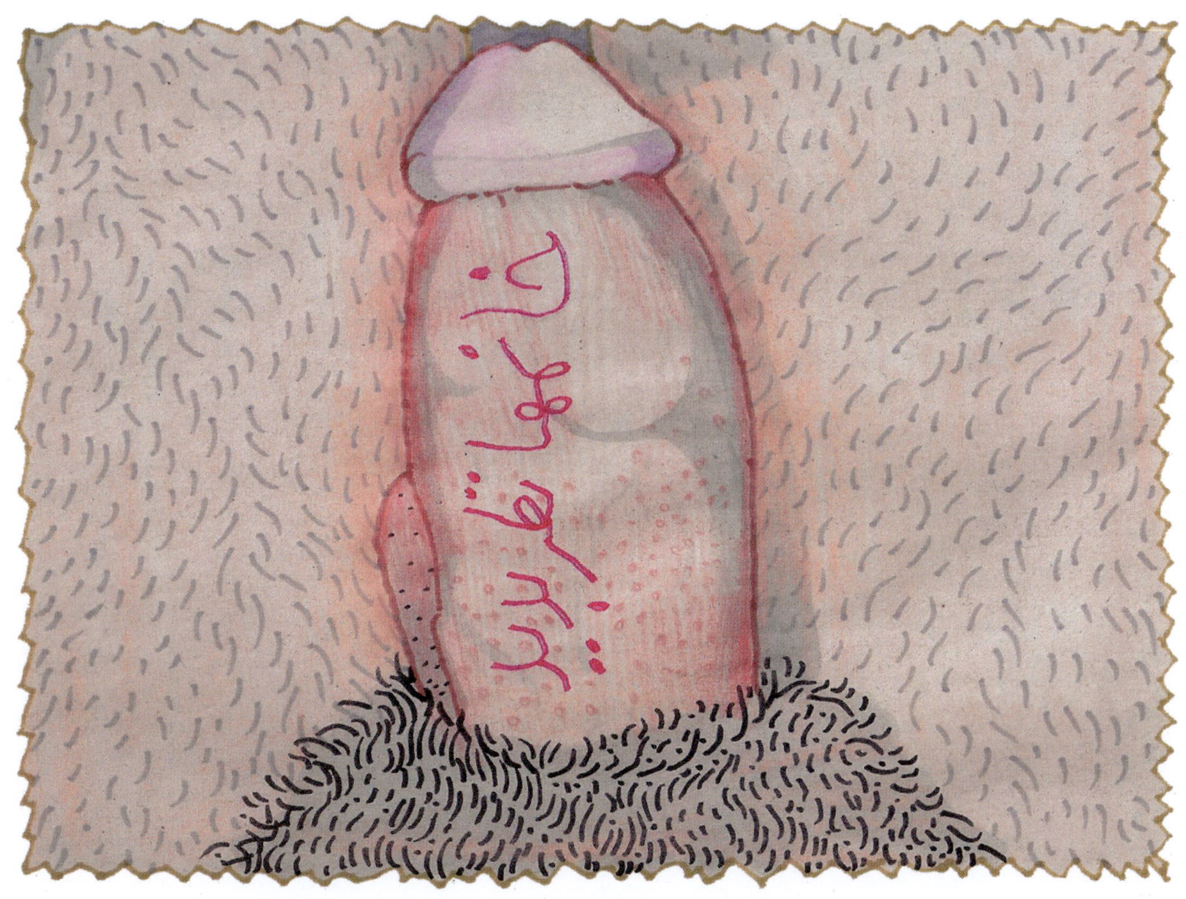

"Ladies, leave your comments"

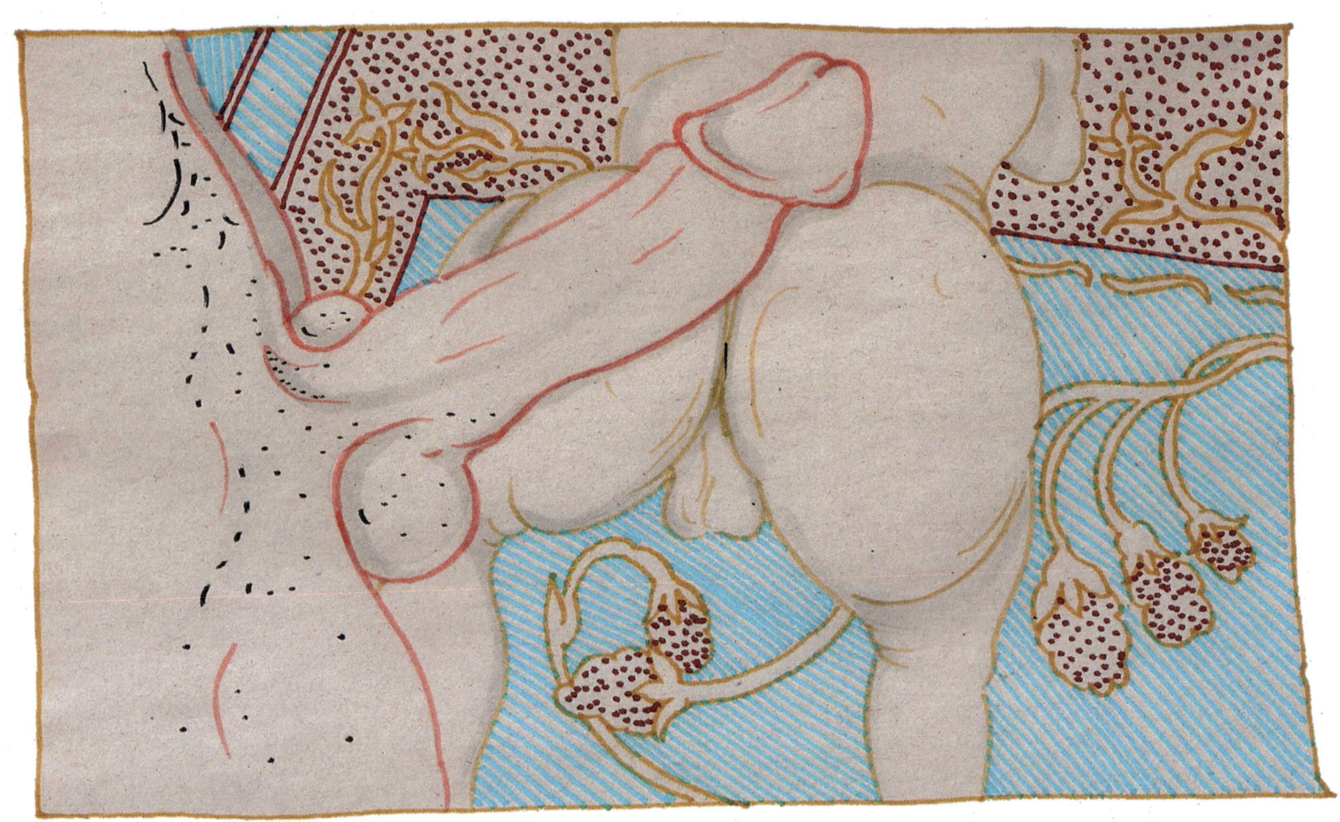

Happy Ending

Printed in Great Britain
by Amazon